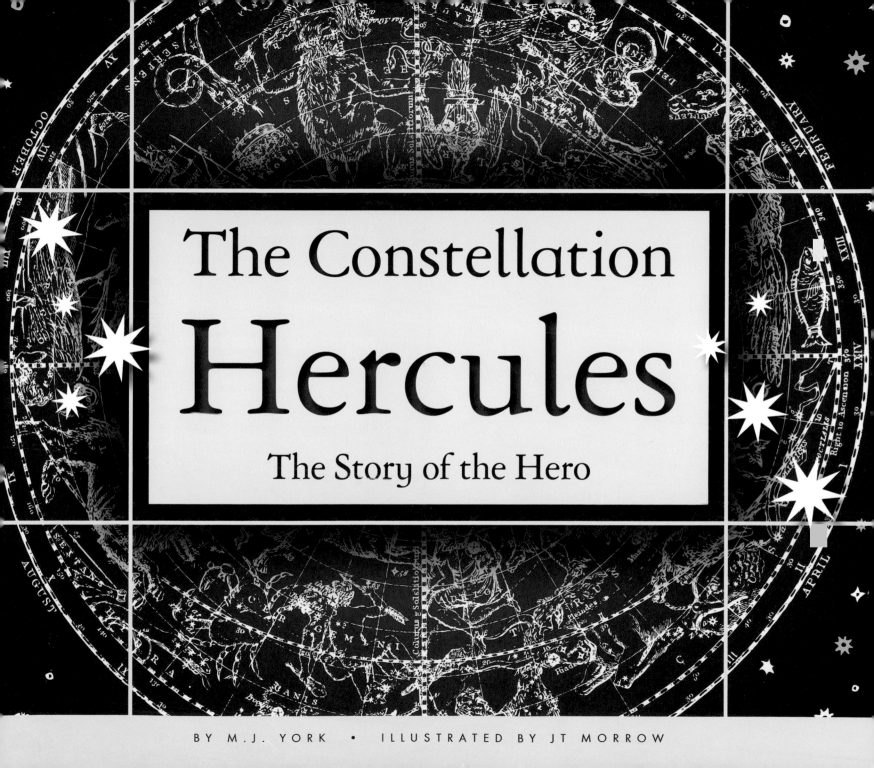

The Constellation
Hercules
The Story of the Hero

BY M.J. YORK • ILLUSTRATED BY JT MORROW

The Child's World

Published by The Child's World®
1980 Lookout Drive • Mankato, MN 56003-1705
800-599-READ • www.childsworld.com

Acknowledgments
The Child's World®: Mary Berendes, Publishing Director
Red Line Editorial: Editorial direction and production
The Design Lab: Design

Photographs ©: Sergey Mikhaylov/Shutterstock Images, 5; iStockphoto/
Thinkstock, 6, 14, 27; Hemera Technologies/Getty Images/Thinkstock,
7; Volkova Anna/Shutterstock Images , 9; Giovanni Benintende/
Shutterstock Images, 10; Dorling Kindersley RF/Thinkstock, 11;
Wikipedia, 13; Library of Congress, 15; Matej Hudovernik/Shutterstock
Images, 16; Vladimir Korostyshevskiy/Shutterstock Images, 17

Design elements: Alisafoytik/Dreamstime

ISBN: 9781623234867
LCCN: 2013931331

Printed in the United States of America
Mankato, MN
July, 2013
PA02168

ABOUT THE AUTHOR

M. J. York is a children's author and editor living in Minnesota. She likes to stargaze on warm summer nights and make up her own constellations.

ABOUT THE ILLUSTRATOR

JT Morrow has worked as a freelance illustrator for more than 20 years and has won several awards. He also works in graphic design and animation. Morrow lives just south of San Francisco, California, with his wife and daughter.

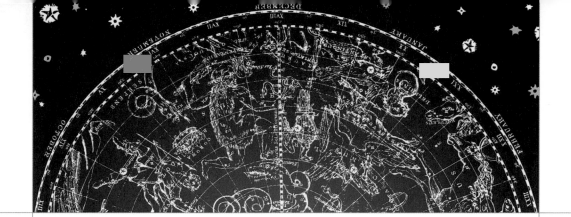

Table of Contents

CHAPTER 1

The Constellation Hercules

Look up at the stars. Connect the dots. What do you see? People have watched the night skies for thousands of years. Ancient people saw patterns in the stars—animals, heroes, and gods. One pattern of stars tells the story of a famous hero: Hercules.

The ancient Greeks called Hercules "Heracles." They told stories of his **legendary** strength. His mother was said to be human but his father was Zeus, the king of the gods. Hercules journeyed

▶ The constellation Hercules shows the hero carrying a club.

around the world, performing impossible tasks and feats of strength. When he died, he rose to live on Mount Olympus, the home of the gods.

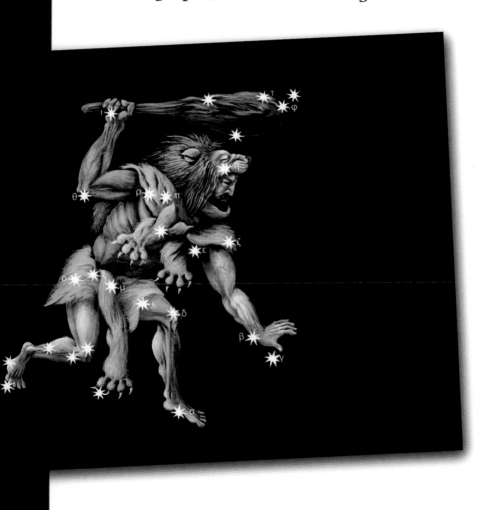

What Is a Star?

Each of the stars in a
constellation is a huge cloud of
gas. Stars put out lots of light
and energy. Most stars are
hundreds of thousands of times
larger than Earth. Most are
trillions of miles away from
us, too. Up to 6,000 stars can
be seen from Earth without a
telescope. But you cannot see
all the stars at once. Some stars are seen
only from the Southern **Hemisphere** and others from
the Northern Hemisphere. Some stars show up in the
winter and others in the summer.

▲ We can see thousands of stars
from Earth.

▶ Opposite page: Modern
astronomers' constellations are
based on ancient Greek ideas.

What Is a Constellation?

The ancient Greeks wrote down the patterns they saw in the night sky. We call these patterns constellations. A constellation is also an area of the sky. It is not just the stars but also the space between and around them.

In 150 AD, the Greek scientist Ptolemy wrote a book that named 48 constellations. Since that time, **astronomers** have added many constellations. Today we recognize 88 constellations.

Stars in Hercules

Hercules is the fifth-largest constellation. But its stars are not very bright. The brightest star in Hercules is his right shoulder. This star is named Beta Herculis. It is also called Kornephoros. This means "club bearer" in Greek. The hero Hercules is known for carrying a club.

The second-brightest star is Hercules's head. This star is named Alpha Herculis. It is also called Rasalgethi. This Arabic word means "head of the kneeling one." An older name for the Hercules constellation, Engonasin, means "the kneeling one."

Other stars mark Hercules's shoulders, arms, body, and legs. Hercules looks upside down in the sky compared to neighboring constellations.

▶ *Opposite page: The stars of Hercules*

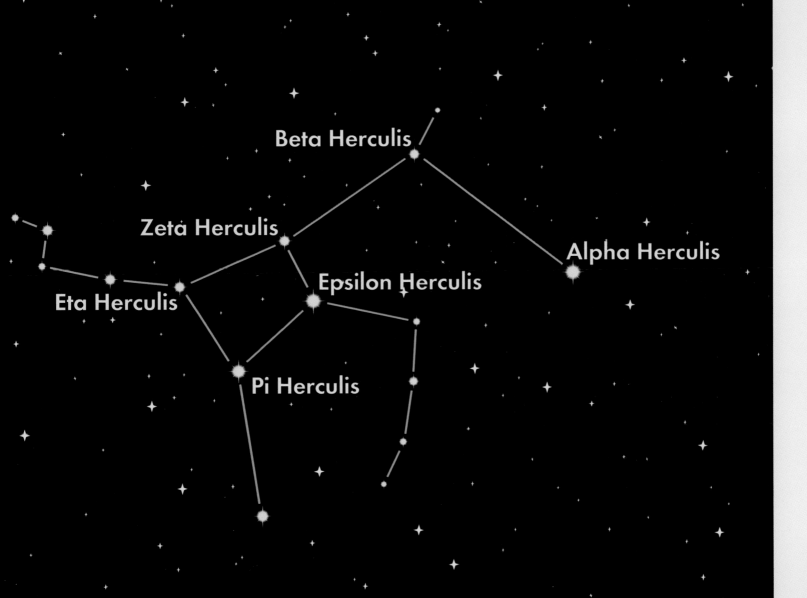

Beta Herculis

Zeta Herculis

Alpha Herculis

Eta Herculis

Epsilon Herculis

Pi Herculis

Star Clusters in Hercules

Astronomers have found clusters of stars and **galaxies** in the Hercules constellation. One is the star cluster M13. It is a group of many stars that are packed close together in a ball. M13 is bright, and you can see it without a telescope. Another star cluster, M92, is a little less bright.

◄ The stars in M13 cluster together.

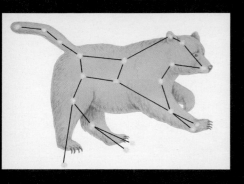

▲ *The Big Dipper in Ursa Major*

Entire galaxies can also cluster together. The Hercules Cluster of galaxies is one of these clusters. It is also called Abell 2151. Over millions of years, these galaxies will move closer together until they eventually merge.

Hercules's Asterism

Hercules also has one **asterism**, called the Keystone asterism. It is a four-sided shape. It makes up Hercules's body. Its four stars are called Epsilon Herculis, Zeta Herculis, Eta Herculis, and Pi Herculis.

CHAPTER 2

The Origin of the Myth of Hercules

The character Hercules or Heracles is part of Greek mythology. As a son of the king of the gods, Zeus, Hercules is a mighty hero. But Hercules's story has many forerunners. Some of the oldest stories ever told are about heroes or people who are part god.

Hercules is similar to the hero Gilgamesh. Gilgamesh was a king in ancient Sumer. He was also part god. Both heroes wore a lion's skin and carried a club. They were both much stronger than other men. Both had to stop a giant bull.

ANCIENT SUMER

The ancient Sumerians lived in Mesopotamia. Today most of this region is in modern Iraq. The Sumerians built some of the first cities in the world. Their rulers were also heads of their religion. Their temples were tall, stepped pyramids called ziggurats.

The Sumerian hero Gilgamesh has much in common with Hercules.

Hercules's Constellation

Hercules's constellation is older than the Greek myths. Early Greeks saw the same shape in the stars. But they called the shape Engonasin, or "the kneeling one." They saw Engonasin on one knee with his arms raised. They believed he was tired from working. But they didn't tell other stories about him. The shape was so ancient even the Greeks weren't sure where its first stories came from. Sometimes they told different stories about these stars, too. Later, the old constellation Engonasin was linked to Hercules and got its new name.

In the sky, Hercules seems to be kneeling on another constellation, Draco. Draco is a dragon or monstrous snake. One of Hercules's feats was to kill a dragon. Some earlier people saw the same story in the stars. The ancient Phoenicians saw Hercules as their sun god, also killing a dragon.

THE PHOENICIANS
The Phoenicians were an ancient people who lived around 1550 BC to 300 BC. They were seafarers and traders who sailed the Mediterranean Sea. They transferred parts of their culture to the Greeks, including their alphabet. The letters we write with today evolved from their alphabet.

▼ *Phoenician writing*

▶ *Opposite page: Hercules kneels upside down in the sky.*

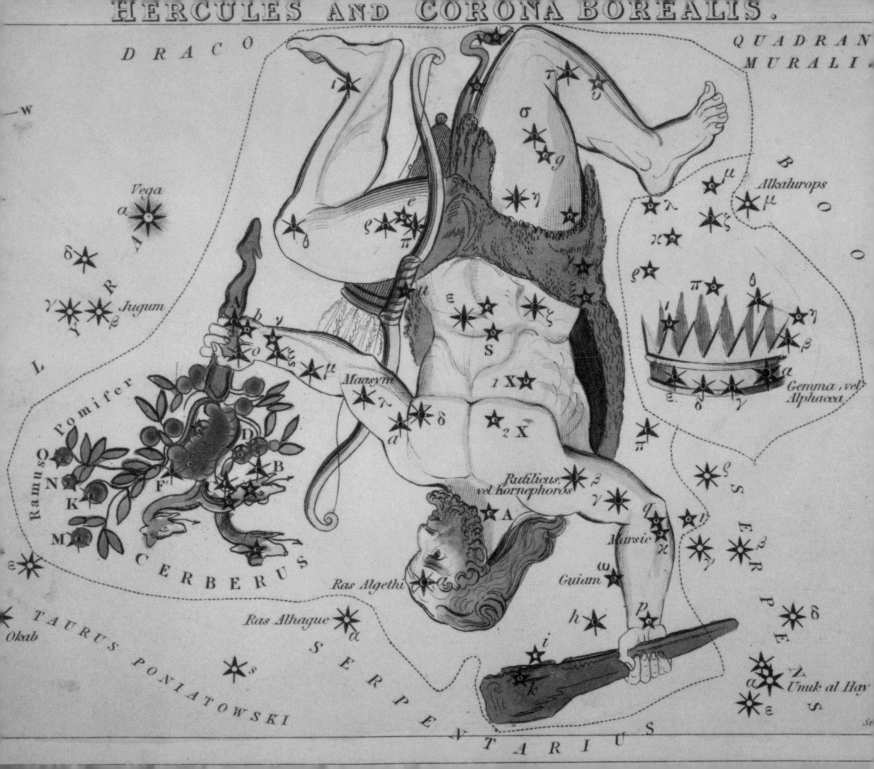

DRACO

QUADRAN
MURALI.

— w

Vega

Alkalurops

B

O

O

δ

R

A

Jugum

γ

β

L

I

R

A

Pomifer

Maasym

Gemma, vel
Alphacca.

Ramus

N

K

M

D

B

F

CERBERUS

Rutilicus,
vel Kornephoros

Marsic

S

E

R

Guiam

P

Ras Algethi

Ras Alhague

α

δ

Okab

TAURUS PONIATOWSKI

SERPENTARIUS

Unuk al Hay

E

N

S

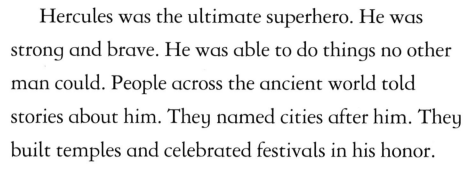

◄ *Opposite page: People across the ancient world built temples to Hercules. This Temple of Hercules is in Amman in modern-day Jordan.*

▼ *Hercules was a favorite god in the ancient world.*

Hercules was the ultimate superhero. He was strong and brave. He was able to do things no other man could. People across the ancient world told stories about him. They named cities after him. They built temples and celebrated festivals in his honor. They **worshipped** him as a god, a protector of humans.

Hercules was a favorite god of many young men. They wanted to be strong and brave like Hercules when they went to war. Many temples to Hercules even had gyms!

CHAPTER 3

The Story of Hercules

Long ago, Zeus was king of the gods of Greece. He wanted to be the father of the greatest king in the world. He chose the beautiful Alcmene to be his hero's mother. Alcmene was the granddaughter of the great hero Perseus. Her son would be a mighty king. After nine months, the child was due to be born. But Hera, Zeus's wife, was angry.

First, Hera made Zeus make a promise. The next child born who was related to Perseus would be king. Zeus knew his son Hercules was about to be born, so he agreed. Hera sprang into action. First, she delayed Zeus's son from being born. Next, she made another baby, Eurystheus, be born early. Eurystheus was also related to Perseus. Since he was born first, Eurystheus became king instead of Hercules.

Zeus's plan was ruined. Now Hercules could not be king. Instead, Zeus bargained with Hera. Hercules would perform 12 tasks for King Eurystheus. When Hercules was finished, he could become a god. Hera agreed. But she was not finished with Hercules.

Alcmene was afraid to raise Hercules. She knew Hera was jealous. And Alcmene was right to worry. Hera was only waiting for the right moment to attack. One night, she sent two giant snakes to kill the baby Hercules. Their poisoned fangs gleamed in the lamp-lit nursery, and their eyes shot beams of

fire. But Hercules was not afraid. He grabbed both snakes, one in each hand, and strangled them. The snakes were dead before his mother could run into the room.

Hercules's first act as a hero happened when he was a teenager. He heard stories of a fearsome lion. The lion had been killing people and animals nearby. Hercules tracked the lion to its lair. He grabbed a branch from an olive tree. With this club he killed the lion. He took the lion's skin and made a cloak. He wore the cloak forever after.

Hera saw that Hercules was doing well. Hercules even had a wife, Megara. Hera was jealous again. This time, she drove Hercules mad. In his madness, Hercules killed people. Megara left him, too.

When he recovered, Hercules felt terrible. He went to see an **oracle**. The oracle told Hercules to visit King Eurystheus. The king would give Hercules 12 impossible tasks. When Hercules finished the tasks, he would be forgiven his crimes. He would also become a god.

Hercules went to King Eurystheus. The king had many dangerous and difficult jobs for Hercules. Hercules had to bring back the skin from an unbeatable lion and kill a flock of man-eating birds. He had to kill a hydra, which is a monster snake with hundreds of heads. He had to bring back a sacred stag, a sacred bull, and a sacred boar. He had to catch a herd of magic oxen and a herd of man-eating horses. He had to fetch a sash from the queen of the Amazons, a fierce group of women warriors. He had to find a magic golden apple. He had to get past a fierce dragon to reach the magic apple. And he had to clean a giant horse stable in just one day. Hercules did all these things.

Finally, Hercules had to bring back the monster Cerberus. Cerberus was a three-headed dog. He guarded the entrance to the underworld.

This was supposed to be the most difficult task. But Hercules was smart. Instead of stealing Cerberus, he asked permission from Hades, the god of the underworld. Hades said yes, and thus Hercules completed his labors.

Afterward, Hercules had many adventures. The goddess Athena watched over him. He helped many people. He even married again. His new wife was Deianeira.

A centaur gave Deianeira a love potion. But the centaur was Hercules's enemy. And the love potion was actually poison. Not knowing the danger, Deianeira gave the potion to Hercules. He was poisoned and he soon died. But when Hercules died, he went to live on Mount Olympus with the other gods. And his shape became a constellation in the night sky.

CHAPTER 4

Hercules in Other Cultures

In China, people saw a **celestial** market in Hercules's stars. Some stars made the walls. Others made a tax office. And still others stood for government officials. At the center of the market, the bright star Alpha Herculis (Rasalgethi) marks the ruler's throne.

The Blackfoot people of the Great Plains see their own legends in the sky. From Hercules's stars, they trace the fingers of Spider Man. Spider Man lived in the sky with the gods. With his fingers, he spun a strong web. He could bring people into the heavens with his webs.

▶ *Where the Greeks saw Hercules, the Chinese saw a market and the Blackfoot saw the fingers of Spider Man.*

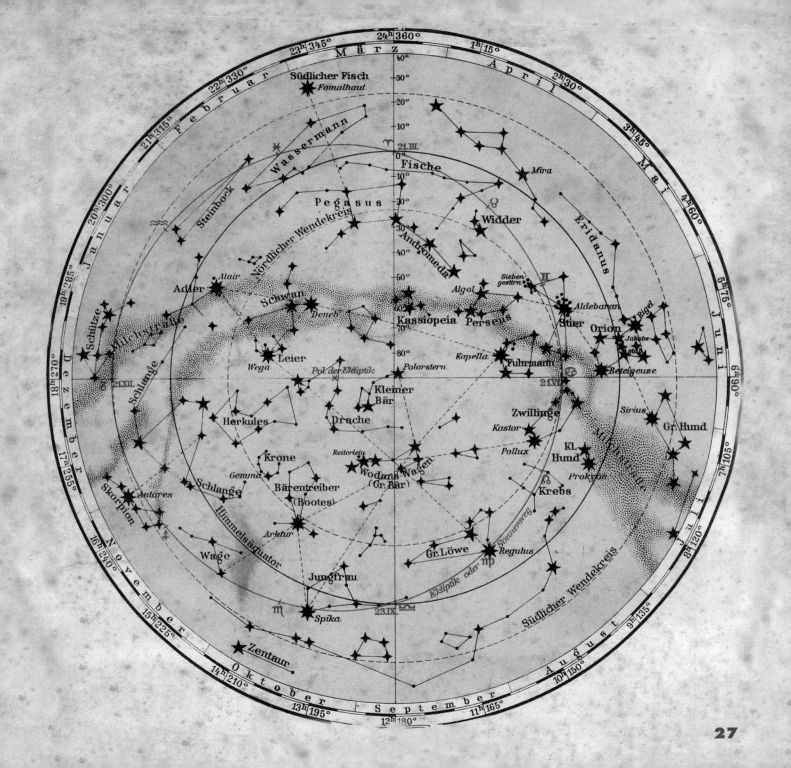

27

CHAPTER 5

How to Find Hercules

The constellation Hercules is faint without a telescope. But you can see the six stars that make his body. In the Northern Hemisphere, look for Hercules in spring. Find the Big Dipper and the Little Dipper. The tail of Draco snakes between these constellations. Follow Draco out to the dragon's head. The dragon is looking right at our hero.

Look at the stars around Hercules. The Greeks saw a swan, a crown, a *lyre*, a dragon, a snake, and a herdsman. What do you see? A house or a cat? A princess or a superhero? What stories can you tell about the stars?

Glossary

asterism (AS-tuh-rih-zem)
An asterism is a well-known group of stars that is smaller than a constellation. The Big Dipper is a famous asterism.

astronomers (uh-STRAW-nuh-murz)
Scientists who study stars and other objects in space are called astronomers. The astronomers discovered a new star.

celestial (suh-LES-chul)
Something celestial has to do with the sky or the stars. Chinese philosophers saw a celestial city in the night sky.

galaxies (GAL-ax-eez)
Groups of millions or billions of stars form galaxies. Some bright lights in the night sky are galaxies.

hemisphere (HEM-uh-spheer)
One half of a planet is one hemisphere. You can see Orion from the northern hemisphere.

legendary (LEJ-uhn-der-ee)
If something is legendary it comes from a story handed down from the past. Stories about Orion are legendary.

lyre (lire)
A lyre is a stringed instrument similar to a harp. The ancient Greeks made music with the lyre.

meteor (MEE-tee-ur)
A meteor is a space rock that burns up in Earth's atmosphere. A meteor makes a streak of light in the night sky as it burns up.

oracle (OR-uh-kuhl)
An oracle is a person who speaks for the gods. The oracle gave Hercules advice.

orbit (OR-bit)
To orbit is to take a round path around something. Eight planets orbit the Sun.

planets (PLAN-its)
Planets are large round objects in space that move around the Sun or another star. Eight planets move around the Sun.

worshipped (WUR-shipt)
If something is worshipped, it is loved and respected as a god. Some ancient Greeks worshipped Hercules.

Learn More

Books

Orr, Tamra. *The Monsters of Hercules*. Hockessin, DE: Mitchell Lane, 2010.

Riordan, James. *The Twelve Labors of Hercules*. London: Frances Lincoln, 2000.

Stott, Carole, and Giles Sparrow. *Starfinder: The Complete Beginner's Guide to Exploring the Night Sky*. New York: DK Publishing, 2010.

Web Sites

Visit our Web site for links about Hercules:

childsworld.com/links

Note to Parents, Teachers, and Librarians:
We routinely verify our Web links to make sure they are safe and active sites. So encourage your readers to check them out!

Index

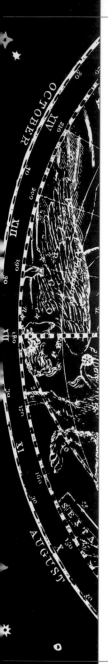